PRAISE FOR THE 3-MINUTE SHOWER RESET

"In The 3-Minute Shower Reset, Jenny Garufi turns a daily ritual into a sacred portal of transformation. With clarity, playfulness, and deep wisdom, she shows you how to shift your mindset, elevate your energy, and connect with your higher self—all in the time it takes to shampoo your hair. This isn't just a book; it's a reset button for your soul. Read it. Practice it. Watch your life change."

—Dr. Joe Vitale, bestselling author of *The Attractor Factor* and star of *The Secret*

"Jenny is a startling proof of the miraculous, and her exercises can offer the same type of phenomenal blessings to you. Wheelchair bound, she married the healing power of water with the mindfulness exercises in this book. The resulting magic healed her. Of course, she applied her muscles to do the deep work but the outcome was... incredible health and a transformed life. Whatever you want to achieve, Jenny's book can help you accomplish that dream in time increments of 3 minute showers taken within 21 days of focus. She's the best. And yes, you deserve to learn from the best!"

—Cyndi Dale, author of 40 books about energy medicine including *Transforming The Legacy*

"This book is an act of devotion disguised as a shower hack. Jenny G doesn't just teach mindfulness—she makes it feel like an absolute homecoming. In The 3-Minute Shower Reset, she offers a gentle yet powerful path for reclaiming your mind, your peace, and your presence—in the most overlooked corners of your life. It's medicine for the soul, served up in the sacred day-to-day. Jenny reminds us that it's not about doing it perfectly. It's about doing it anyway. Genius.

—Corin Grillo, Best-Selling Author of *The Angel Experiment* and *Angel Wealth Magic*

"I just read Jenny Garufi's new book The 3-Minute Shower Reset and it was life-changing. I have been meditating for decades, and one of the issues I have struggled with is consistency. I could find any excuse to not meditate. What Jenny has done with this book is give us a way to be not only consistent, but also to offer real practices and methods to stay on track with meditation. She also reminds us meditation does not look the same for everyone. She breaks down this very simple way to enhance a practice you may already have, and it also offers an easy path for people who have felt that meditation is just too hard for them to accomplish. The book offers truly practical methods of utilizing moments that you would have already carved out for uninterrupted time making it intentional for meditation. She gives step-by-step processes that are so easy to incorporate into your everyday routine. She makes mindfulness

and meditation accessible to everyone. The book itself is just so enjoyable to read. Jenny has been on the forefront of the mindfulness space for decades and offers true expertise on every page. Throughout the book are personal stories and recollections of how she has used these techniques successfully for herself and her clients. I am already seeing a change within my own mindfulness journey after devouring this book. It's truly a game changer for anyone interested in meditation."

—Amy Loughren, RN, Master NLP Practitioner, The real nurse from the Netflix movie *The Good Nurse*

"As a psychiatrist who works with older individuals and those with chronic and often complex medical conditions, I am always looking for non-pharmacological tools with the ability to maximally harness wellness. What Jenny has provided with this book is exactly that and so much more. She shares a powerful tool that supports moving from a state of dis-ease to a plane of ease. The bonus is that this does not carry risk for side effects in the way that all medications potentially do. This is one of those 'game changer' books that can bring us all significant wellness wins! Thank you Jenny for this gift!"

—Dr. Sandy Vale, Board certified adult psychiatrist

The 3-Minute Shower Reset

21 DAYS TO INNER PEACE

JENNY GARUFI

FOREWORD BY **DITTE YOUNG**
FEATURED ON THE TELEPATHY TAPES

Jennifer Garufi
The 3-Minute Shower Reset: 21 Days to Inner Peace

Emerging Light Books
Copyright © 2025 by Jennifer Garufi
First Edition

Softcover ISBN 979-8-9993540-0-6
eBook ISBN 979-8-9993540-1-3
Audiobook ISBN 979-8-9993540-2-0

Book Design | Ashley Russell Designs
Editor | Kathie Lynas
Author Portrait Photographer | Jessica Marx
Publishing Management | TSPA The Self Publishing Agency, Inc.

This book is dedicated to all my fellow recovering
perfectionists and people pleasers.
It is also dedicated to anyone struggling through these
rapidly changing times.
May you find a soft exhale here — a moment to pause, to
breathe, and to remember that you are already enough.
For everyone learning to slow down,
to put down distractions,
to meet themselves with compassion,
and to turn simple moments into sacred ones.
May these pages guide you gently back to yourself — to
the peace that lives in the present moment
to the love that's been waiting within,
and to the quiet joy of showing up just as you are.
From my heart to yours,
Jenny

CONTENTS

FOREWORD
BY DITTE YOUNG

In a world saturated with noise, urgency, and distractions, the sacred art of silence has become a rare and precious gift. As a telepath, clairvoyant, and profoundly intuitive soul, I have come to understand through personal experience and spiritual insight that silence is not merely the absence of sound. It is a gateway to self-awareness, healing, and inner clarity. At the heart of this journey lies the practice of cleansing, not only of the physical body but of the energetic and emotional layers that so often become cluttered by the weight of our lives.

Cleansing is more than a ritual of hygiene. A clean body invites clean energy, and from that energy, a clean soul emerges. It is no coincidence that so many ancient spiritual traditions begin with water — baptisms, purifications, and, sacred baths. Water is a carrier, a cleanser, and a healer. When I step into the shower, I am not just washing away the dust of the day. I am resetting my system, releasing energies that no longer serve me, and grounding myself in the present moment. As the water runs over my skin, I turn my attention inward. My thoughts grow quiet. My breathing slows. My inner world lights up.

It is in these moments of intentional stillness that I reconnect with myself. I close my eyes and allow my inner vision to awaken. I see images, receive messages, and feel emotions rise and fall like gentle waves. I allow myself to dream, to manifest, or to listen. Water becomes my portal — an entryway into presence, into truth.

There is profound wisdom in the element of water. It is both powerful and soft, cleansing and calming. When life becomes chaotic — when emotions like anger, stress, or sadness cloud my clarity — I visualize water. I feel its cooling embrace in my imagination, and like a river washing over stone, it smooths the edges of my mind and heart. It reminds me that everything can be softened. Everything can be transformed.

When we invite stillness into our lives, when we become quiet, we become clear.

In that clarity, we stop projecting our pain onto others. We stop assuming, blaming, reacting. Instead, we begin to feel. We begin to see. We recognize the sacredness of the people around us, and we treat them with more kindness, more patience, more empathy. True empathy is born from this quiet place — when our minds no longer scream with judgment or fear, and we can finally hear the voices of other souls.

In this book, you will be invited to explore the deep connection between cleansing, silence, and spiritual presence. You will be guided not just to clean your body but to purify your thoughts, calm your emotions, and listen to the whispers of your soul. You will learn how to use water as a spiritual ally. Not only as a physical necessity but as a tool for grounding, resetting, and returning to your most authentic self.

In our fast-paced world, this return is not a luxury — it is essential. We must remember how to feel. We must remember how to *be*. Empathy, connection, and peace. These are not abstract ideals. They are born in the quiet spaces of our daily lives. And they begin with a single, simple act: turning inward.

May this book be your companion on the path to a more profound presence, gentler living, and greater connection — not only with yourself but with the world around you. May the element of water, in all its silent wisdom, teach you to soften, to listen, and to cleanse not just your body but your soul.

—Ditte Young, Telepath, Author, Animal Communicator, Therapist, featured on *The Telepathy Tapes* and TEDx Speaker

PROLOGUE
THE JOURNEY THAT BROUGHT ME HERE

As a recovering perfectionist, people pleaser, and someone who healed her physical body through her mind — boy, do I knew about mindfulness! I have seen exercises such as the ones I include in this book change my own life and the lives of the thousands of people I have been blessed to work with. Tapping into mindfulness and presence allowed me to heal myself of seven years of chronic disease and pain, in three weeks. Adopting some of these exercises allowed me to manifest a book deal with a top publisher. Studying the power of mindfulness brought me my husband, who is the love of my life. I have been with him for eleven years, and it just keeps getting better. Consistently practicing these exercises has allowed me to have happy and healthy relationships with my kids, my husband's kids, friends, loved ones, and clients.

Working with thousands of clients over the past twenty years, through one-on-one work, giving readings, and facilitating workshops and classes has given me deep insight into our similarities as well as the challenges we share. By adopting some of these easy exercises into our daily routines — our lives can shift, and we can move beyond previous limitations. We tend to repeat our own limitations, but it is not from a conscious state. It is not like we are looking to self-sabotage; it is usually our ego trying to keep ourselves safe, since *any* change can be seen as a threat. When we learn to truly listen to ourselves instead of being on automatic pilot, our lives transform.

Let me take you back to a little over twenty years ago. By that time, I had been struggling with severe pain every day for seven years. Most of my pain was in my legs, but I hurt in almost every part of my body.

Over that period, doctors had diagnosed me with four different chronic diseases, one of which was a genetic blood disorder called Factor V Leiden. My medical team told me this condition made it probable I would develop a blood clot, and sure enough, I manifested one within a month of being told this.

My last prognosis had the doctors telling me I would wind up in a wheelchair, potentially within a year. My days were gripped by unrelenting pain and fear about the future that awaited me. Would I be able to drive my kids anywhere or otherwise take care of them, or would I pass out from the pain, or have to crawl down the stairs? I was constantly beating myself up about not being able to be the mom, wife, friend, daughter, and person that I desired to be.

I was continually seeking answers from both traditional and alternative sources. Mainstream doctors offered more diagnoses and prescriptions but no hope for a cure. I went to a naturopath who wanted me on 30 vitamins a day. Keeping track of the vitamin regimen caused extra stress and anxiety, as each vitamin needed to be taken at a certain time — with or without food or alongside another vitamin. I read a book that said to have a "funeral for my old self" and to make peace with the reality that I would never have a quality of life I was used to or desired.

I was in support groups that were not supportive. Instead, they felt like a "one-upping" of how bad life was and how many medications everyone was on. I went to a chiropractor three times a week, which did offer periods of temporary relief.

I lived seven years like this!! Most days, all I could focus on was how much the pain hurt. Pain is attention-getting and can take over our perception of the world. It was not until I began listening to myself that I began to hear my harmful inner monologue. I could not possibly heal from that space.

Paying closer attention to my body and mind and how I spoke to my body led me on a pursuit of answers. These new approaches all required me to start paying attention to my thoughts and embrace mindfulness. There were a few catalysts to my physical healing. The first was hearing about writing gratitude lists.

I had always loved to write. While I was sick, writing became a way to "vent" and complain about how bad everything was. Once I started focusing on some things that made me smile, on what I was grateful for, I felt an opening in my heart.

The second catalyst was meeting my friend Angela (truly

an angel, heaven-sent). When I met her, we became instant friends. I had refused pain pills until that point as I was terrified of becoming addicted. When I met Angela, I would take a quarter of the recommended dose so I could have the ability to go for walks with her. Those walks and talks had me remembering who Jenny was, not just "sick Jenny." I was grateful the pills allowed me to remember what it was like to actually be pain free. I was and am forever grateful to Angela for the love and non-judgment she offered, which allowed me to see myself differently.

The final and biggest catalyst was seeing the movie, *The Secret,* and taking a few messages away from it: 1) The body is always creating cells. What we are telling ourselves and especially, the energy and emotion with which we are saying it, inform the cells whether they should be healthy or sick. 2) Gratitude heals.

I didn't have room for gratitude because I was so focused on the pain and all I could not do and show up for. I had already started writing a little about gratitude, but seeing the movie made it clearer how integral it was to feel gratitude as often as I could. Gratitude was the number-one tool that helped me heal, which is why I take such a deep dive into it in this book.

It took three weeks of focusing on gratitude. It involved watching and reading inspiring materials and truly focusing on my thoughts to heal myself physically. When I healed myself, it took a while for me to go back to doctors. I was off all medications except for blood thinners, which were monitored. When I finally went to my hematologist a year after healing, he gave me his blessing to stop taking them, as I was doing so well. It's been twenty years without a blood clot and without pain.

I mentioned I had horrendous self-talk. Being a perfectionist and people pleaser will do that! How we speak to ourselves usually comes from past relationships, experiences, and often, trauma. You may remember when you did something and proclaimed to yourself, "Oh that was dumb," or maybe you repeat something like "I'm not good at math," "I could never be smart enough to learn that," or "I am horrible at any relationships." When you begin listening and changing how you speak to yourself, the world around you begins to change. You feel better and more positive, and are able to connect with how you *truly* feel instead of repeating some long-expired limiting statement.

I always found being by water and in the shower a place of deep relaxation. Growing up in New York City (NYC), whenever I was stressed, I headed a few blocks away to the East River to gain some sort of peace. When I was healing and had the energy to get to the river near where I was living in upstate New York, I found being there helped messages and relaxation come in to my consciousness. While I was gathering inspirational materials in my three weeks of healing, I learned about the healing qualities of water and its power through Japanese researcher Masaru Emoto.

I was blown away by Emoto's work on the imprints our thoughts and words make on water. Emoto's research visually captured the structure of water at the moment of freezing, and through microscopic photography, he showed the direct consequences of destructive thoughts and of thoughts of love and appreciation on the formation of water crystals.

A glass of water that has positive words spoken to it, like "love" or "gratitude," will make beautiful patterns under a microscope. A glass of water that has negative words spoken to it, words like "hate" or "despair," creates very ugly-looking crystal patterns.

As we are about 55 to 60 percent made up of water, it simply makes sense that how we speak to ourselves affects us. During my three-week healing journey, the shower became an important time for me to do my mindfulness exercises and check in with myself.

After overcoming my physical healing, the next huge healing journey I needed to take was to rise above the grief of losing my mom. My mom was my best friend, greatest supporter, and someone I spoke to every day. She was my example of unconditional love, and when she passed, it truly felt like my heart was ripped out.

After I lost her, I was led to a deeper dive into studying shamanism to connect with the elements and ancestor energy. I found a teacher, Karen Johnson, who offered a class on transmuting grief through shamanism, and it was priceless. This study of shamanism led me to an even deeper appreciation of the magical element of water. Water took on a whole new power. Many ideas for poems and articles have come to me in the shower, as well as guidance and a deep sense of peace. In fact, many of these exercises came from inspiration in the shower! When we combine mindfulness with the water in the shower it truly can equate to what feels like magic. We invite in more peace. We tell ourselves we are worth that attention. We start to move away from our past selves and more into our potential selves.

I have seen thousands of clients change their lives with little shifts. They are always amazed and very grateful. I wanted to share this with more people during this time of great change and serious challenges on our planet. I am sure you have noticed things all over the world are shifting. There is a lot of separation and polarization, with people expressing hostility toward others with different ideas and opinions. There is concern over environmental changes, and governments and other institutions are struggling. Meanwhile, artificial intelligence (AI) is extending its reach into almost every industry and aspect of our lives.

When we become more mindful, we are able to tune into our intuition and discern truth easier. In this age of AI and separation, I can think of nothing more powerful than accessing our intuition, truth and connection. This book will open the door for all of these to come into your life, creating new possibilities and more ease.

Disclaimers:

Safety Precautions

This is a mindfulness practice, so it's important to be aware of how your body feels. The shower has hard surfaces — if you ever feel even slightly dizzy, please sit or lie down. Remember, water has power. Always be mindful of your physical sensations. Feeling calm, peaceful, and relaxed is wonderful. However, feeling dizzy or disoriented is not. If you start to experience these feelings, stop the exercise immediately and move into a position where you feel safe and secure, ensuring you won't fall.

This work is offered as self-work. Not everyone will experience these exercises the same. Be gentle with yourself as you work through them. If things come up that you feel you need help with — reach out to a professional or loved one for help.

Client Stories

I have worked with thousands of clients one-on-one and through my classes. I refer to clients in this book, but *all* of the names have been changed. I have often seen several clients that have similar "stories" and backgrounds, and sometimes the anecdotes are composites of various people's experiences. I honor all privacy working with clients.

Medications

The practices in this book are meant to support your well-being, not replace medical care. Please speak with your doctor before making any changes to medications or treatments — they're part of your healing team too.

INTRODUCTION
HOW TO GET THE MOST OUT OF YOUR SHOWER MINDFULNESS PRACTICE

One of the most common forms of resistance I've encountered to having a mindfulness practice is the excuse, "I have no time for that." I understand that we're all busy, but mindfulness doesn't require extra time. It's a choice we can make in any moment. Mindfulness grants us peace virtually instantaneously. For nearly two decades, I've told my clients that the three most powerful times for mindfulness exercises are before bed, right when you wake up, and in the shower. The shower is typically the one time most of us have to ourselves, and it also offers the healing power of water.

It was in the shower that this idea was born, and writing this book has been an absolute joy. Whenever I sat down to write — whether for two minutes or an hour — the words flowed through me, just waiting to be put on the page. To me, this is a clear sign that it was the right time for this book. In an age full of distractions, I hope this book gives you permission to take some time for yourself. Even after just a few days of practicing these exercises, I believe you will begin to notice changes in your life that will allow it to unfold in new and exciting ways.

This is all a part of my life's journey to help others, and for that, I am deeply honored and grateful. Thank you for being with me on this journey. It is my hope that this book gives you a deeper connection with self and empowers you. Sending you so much love!

Before You Begin

It is said that it takes 21 days to rewire the brain for a new habit. This book offers 21 exercises to help you get started, making your shower time and mindfulness a habit in your life. The shower provides the perfect opportunity to make mindfulness a daily practice. Most of us can take three minutes in the shower to focus our attention. Those three minutes can invite in inner peace and change your day when you intend it to! This is an excellent way to begin if you are new to mindfulness, and it is also a great way to deepen an existing practice, offering new exercises to help you quiet your mind.

What is a Reset and Why Do I Need It?

We often run through our day on automatic pilot. If you are living your best life in every area — emotionally, physically, mentally, spiritually, in all relationships and financially — GOOD for you! Your automatic pilot is stellar, and you obviously have done much inner work. The truth is most of us have one or more areas not in balance. Spending these three minutes in the shower being mindful and learning to direct the mind is life-changing. It is the beginning of a mindfulness practice. It is a re-setting of your energy and attention, which manifests itself into your reality. Mindfulness is the practice of being aware and present in each moment. It means not allowing your thoughts, self-talk, past stories, or trauma to control your day. Instead, you regain control and become conscious of how your life is unfolding.

As you begin to practice mindfulness, the world starts to shift. You learn to respond instead of react. You may realize that instead of being your biggest cheerleader, you've been your harshest critic. Perhaps you've been living in a "Groundhog Day" scenario in one or more areas of your life. Achieving mindfulness isn't difficult, but it does require some time and focus. It's not something that happens overnight but is an ongoing opportunity to be present in every moment. Please be gentle with yourself as you become more mindful.

Why Practice Mindfulness in the Shower?

Most people shower daily, or nearly so, which makes it a convenient way to establish a mindfulness routine and create a habit. Many claim they don't have time for meditation or mindfulness practices, but this is time you already have when you're alone — perfect for connecting more deeply with yourself.

Often, during "shower time," we're lost in thoughts about our "to-do list," operating half-consciously. This new practice helps you reclaim that time. Most of these exercises can be done in one to three minutes during the shower, and many can be adapted for out of the shower. You will see quickly how using these short periods of time can easily switch your mood and invite in a state of inner peace and calm. Most people shower either in the morning or at night — powerful times for setting intentions. During these times, our subconscious mind is especially receptive, being closer to sleep. Water itself is a healing element, so embracing it and utilizing it can enhance your mindfulness practice.

This doesn't require extra time or wasting water — you're simply making the most of resources you're already using!

How to Use This Book

There is no single "right way" to use this book. I encourage you to be intuitive and adapt the exercises in the way that works best for you. This is about making your shower time a mindfulness practice. If you find exercises that resonate with you, consider bookmarking those pages for easy reference. You might choose to focus on one exercise for several days to deepen your experience. This journey is about starting and maintaining a mindfulness practice in the shower, and it will be more sustainable if it feels fun and easy. Remember, if you use this consecutively for 21 days, you are rewiring your brain, and the practice will be easier to maintain. But, please do not beat yourself up if you miss a day. You can always resume tomorrow!

Here Are Four Ways to Approach These Exercises:

1. Follow the book from front to back.

    If this method resonates with you, you'll notice some exercises build on others, while some overlap. Feel free to elaborate on the exercises to make them your own.

2. Pick exercises based on your needs.

    You might prefer to choose exercises based on the chapter headings. One day, you might feel drawn to an exercise focused on the actual water, while another day, you may crave something related to gratitude. Honor yourself by choosing what feels best in the moment.

3. Let spontaneity guide you.

    You could randomly open the book to a page each day and let that exercise choose you. It can be fun to see what you land on, and let spontaneity and chance guide your practice. Alternatively, you could pick a number and turn to that page — you might be surprised by the synchronicity of the exercises chosen this way.

4. Focus on a specific chapter.

    If a particular chapter resonates with you, spend time with it. For example, if you are feeling really sad, focusing on gratitude can truly help to shift that feeling. Spending a few days or practicing that same exercise a few times during that same day (including out of the shower) can help that energy shift faster.

Setting the Intention for Mindfulness Time

If you want to make your entire morning routine in the bathroom your mindfulness practice time, declare that intention. Here's what that might look like:

Before stepping into the shower, look in the bathroom mirror and commit to this time. You might even say an affirmation, such as "I love you. I'm taking this time for you."

Mirror work is a powerful mindfulness tool in its own right. Many of these exercises can be adapted to do in front of the mirror (as long as they don't specifically involve water, or you can incorporate the bathroom sink). If it feels right, integrate mirror work into your routine to deepen your practice. But for now, let the magic of mindfulness begin in the shower!

After the Shower

Always thank yourself for taking the time! If possible, take a few minutes after your shower to jot down any insights that came to you. Whether or not you write anything down, be sure to thank yourself for your time, energy, and remembering to show up for yourself!

Chapter 1
Gratitude

Exercises and Practices (1-9)

The Magic and Power of Gratitude

Gratitude is truly a magical force, capable of transforming energy. It is also one of the simplest ways to cultivate mindfulness. By combining love with appreciation — both of which hold high vibrations — you shift your focus away from where it often lingers: the past, the future, or the negative. Instead, you claim the present moment, taking time to acknowledge and give thanks for the good that exists right now.

You might not always be consciously aware of this, but you have the ability to feel high and low vibrations. Tuning into the beauty, love and gratitude you have had or currently have in your life allows you to feel high vibrations. Going down the rabbit hole of fear, lack, or stress brings on feelings of low vibrations. Our life flows much better when we are in a high vibrational state.

We've all had experiences of both low and high vibrational environments and states of mind.

A low vibration may hit you when you walk into a room and can feel the sadness "in the air." It might occur when you feel down and out about a challenge in your life and find it tough to get out of a funk, or it could be a day when you stub your toe, or spill your coffee, declare it a "horrible day" and then things seem to go downhill from there.

High vibrations are those moments of joy or inner peace. They may occur when we experience a sunrise or other beautiful moment in nature, a long laugh, a pleasant surprise. When we are operating in this state, we can truly feel like we are on top of the world and nothing can go wrong. My husband and I have a running joke in our home. We play a lot of board games, and we both know if I've had a *truly* amazing high-vibration day — there is no way he will beat me at any game! Sounds kind of funny but it's the truth!

Gratitude is an instant connection to a high vibration. It has the power to profoundly shift your perspective, and there are countless ways to invite it into your life. It's said that the average person has around 60,000 thoughts a day, with 80 percent of them being negative and 95 percent being the same thoughts as the day before. Practicing gratitude disrupts this cycle and shifts your energy. When you begin a daily gratitude practice, you will quickly feel changes in your life. Any of the following exercises are powerful — try them all if you can, or start with the ones that resonate most with you. You can always return to the others later. Trust what feels easiest for you in this moment. The more you build momentum with this practice, the more natural it will become.

For each exercise in this book, I will first explain the background and why this exercise holds power for resetting our state of mind. I will then discuss the practice, which is where you will be gaining knowledge about the steps and guidance on how to practice the exercise.

EXERCISE #1
QUALITIES YOU ARE GRATEFUL FOR IN YOURSELF

It's all too common for people to berate themselves, yet few take the time to truly appreciate the wonderful qualities they possess. Every single person has beautiful qualities worth focusing on. The fact that you're reading this book shows that you're interested in inviting in more inner peace and mindfulness. This alone is a great starting point for your gratitude practice.

I know you have many more qualities to be grateful for. Think of the times you've shown kindness, compassion, or love — whether to people, animals, or the planet. Perhaps you check in on those who need extra love or support. Maybe you enjoy cooking, dancing, singing, drawing, or other hobbies. You can also give yourself credit for the way you show up in any relationship, including the one with yourself. Perhaps you're a dedicated worker and a nurturing parent, sibling, spouse, or friend. Maybe you've made meals for others or supported someone in a time of need. You might enjoy mental challenges like crosswords, board games, or puzzles, or love problem-solving. When you practice gratitude toward yourself, you empower yourself instead of disempowering yourself. Starting or ending your day with self-gratitude will create noticeable shifts in your energy.

I have had many clients so beat down by negative messages from parents, family members, partners, or teachers that they found it very hard to focus on something good within themselves. I know when I was ill, it was much easier to tap into what I could not do and was not grateful for, rather than what I was still good at in my life. When I began to actively turn my attention to gratitude for myself — my love of my kids and my desire to take care of myself — my body was finally able to begin to heal itself.

After being published by Llewellyn in 2016, I was hyper-critical of myself. My book wasn't reaching as many people as I had wanted, and I was struggling and taking it very personally. I was on a call with a mentor, and they asked me if I was giving myself credit for writing the book. I was definitely *not*! He suggested that I spend ten minutes thanking myself for the dedication of writing and for this book helping others. Well, I will tell you I was bawling because it was so uncomfortable to give myself this credit. I taught others about gratitude and still obviously had more lessons to learn!

PRACTICE:

We are used to being hard on ourselves. I taught this stuff and was still hypercritical of myself. If you've had a rough upbringing or difficult past relationships, giving yourself gratitude might feel very foreign. Please give yourself some love for that. Are you kind? Do you care about other beings be they human, plants or animals? You are reading this book, which means you have a desire to make your life easier. *All* of these are amazing qualities to be grateful to yourself for.

While in the shower, bring to mind a quality or qualities you appreciate about yourself. You can do this while standing under the stream of water or as you wash. Focus on one or more of these qualities for as long as you can, even recalling moments when you demonstrated them. Give yourself credit and gratitude for having these qualities. You may want to notice if you feel that gratitude in any part of your body. There is no set time for this — any amount is beneficial. The more you practice, the more natural it will become. Challenge yourself to stay in this space of self-gratitude for a few minutes, then gradually longer. You'll feel the internal shift! Thank yourself for noticing a quality you are grateful for in yourself.

EXERCISE #2
CHALLENGES AND LIFE SITUATIONS YOU ARE GRATEFUL FOR OVERCOMING

It's easy to get caught up in the challenges of the present moment, so much so that you may forget just how much you've already overcome to be where you are today. You've faced challenges, whether within yourself, with loved ones, in your career, or with your health. Most likely, you've had to overcome several of these obstacles. Perhaps you've experienced grief, trauma, or loss; yet, you are here today, choosing to become a more mindful version of yourself. Each challenge, no matter how insurmountable it seemed, you made it through. That deserves a lot of credit. Maybe you've left a tough relationship, dealt with grief, or overcome childhood trauma. Perhaps you've endured a toxic work environment, struggled with health issues, or battled anxiety or depression. You might have watched loved ones go through their own struggles. When you give yourself credit for overcoming these challenges, you're not only acknowledging your strength, fortitude, and resilience, but you're also empowering yourself to know that whatever challenge you're facing now will also pass.

When my mom passed, I truly felt like my heart broke into pieces. She was my best friend and my biggest cheerleader, and I spoke with her every day of my 50 years of life, often more than once a day. Her leaving left a hole, but I knew I had to move forward and that she would want me to do so. Grief took several different roads and was not by any means a straight path. It led to me starting a daily meditation practice, which has now been part of my life for over four years. I was trying to fill the void of our morning calls, and it set me more firmly on my path of healing. I can feel gratitude for myself for moving forward when I did not feel I could.

During my last twenty years of working with clients as a mentor and guide, I have seen women leave abusive marriages, witnessed people move on from jobs they could not stand, and have seen people overcome hardships that many would have been paralyzed by. If you are on this planet, you have overcome. That deserves gratitude.

PRACTICE:

Whether it be grief you have moved through, leaving a job or relationship not serving your highest good, or another way you have overcome … recognize that these deserve celebration and gratitude for making it to the other side!

While under the stream of water or as you wash, bring to mind a time when you were proud of yourself for over-coming a challenge or managing a difficult situation. You might also recall a moment when you stood up for yourself or another time you made yourself proud. As you hold that memory, close your eyes and truly feel the sense of relief and accomplishment for having overcome that challenge. Congratulate yourself. Stay in this feeling for as long as you're comfortable, and if you want, bring in another memory. This practice is about sinking into gratitude for yourself — for your strength and your resilience. Take a moment to give yourself a hug for recognizing and honoring your journey.

EXERCISE #3
THINGS OR PLACES YOU ARE GRATEFUL FOR

People often focus on what they don't have and what they want, which sends out an energy of lack. This energy inevitably draws more feelings of scarcity into your life. However, when you shift your focus to what you do have, that energy is amplified. In my journey of physical healing, when I began focusing on things like my comfortable bed and warm showers, it genuinely changed how I felt. Having food in your fridge, a bed to sleep in, or clothes to wear may be things you've grown accustomed to, but many people don't have these basic comforts.

People also tend to complain about where they live: their apartment or house, the city, the state, the country, and the world in general. But there are always reasons to be grateful for where you live. After all, you've met people there, have some of your favorite belongings, have felt the safety of having walls around you, have seen beautiful things outside, and know the world as a whole offers countless wonders.

Do you have a favorite food? A favorite shirt? Do you love the feeling of your bed, pillows, and blankets at night? What can you find to be grateful for about your home, your town, state, country, or the world as a whole?? Focusing on these small comforts can spark a deep sense of gratitude.

I had a client, "Alicia," who had suffered a ton of abuse from her mom and from other relationships, and she had a pretty hard time tapping into gratitude. Alicia admitted she was a "Debbie Downer" but had found herself a victim so often in life — it was hard to find anything to be grateful for. I remember being brought to tears when she came into a session saying she stopped on the side of the road when driving to take in a sunset. She said she felt gratitude through every cell of her body and felt something shift within. She remembered what it was like to feel that joy, and that made it easier for her to find it again.

PRACTICE:

Even Alicia, who had endured so much abuse throughout decades of her life, was overcome with gratitude for a sunset. I am sure there is at least one thing or place that comes to mind that you can truly feel into and experience gratitude for. The deeper you tap into the feelings of gratitude, the more magical it truly is.

While under the stream of water or as you wash, bring to mind one or a few things you are grateful for. If it's a favorite food, try to recall its taste, texture, and the satisfaction it brings. If it's your bed, imagine how it feels on your skin when you slide under the covers, totally relaxed. Engage your senses as you bring these thoughts to mind and say, "thank you." If you'd like to expand this exercise, tune into each sense:

- Think of a taste you are grateful for.
- Picture something that makes you smile whenever you see it.
- Recall a smell that you love and feel grateful for.
- Think of something that brings you comfort and gratitude when you touch it.
- Remember a sound that fills you with peace and gratitude.

I bet you'll find yourself smiling during and after this exercise. Embrace those smiles — they are healing — and express gratitude for life just as it is, right in this moment. Thank yourself for taking this time.

EXERCISE #4
"BEINGS" YOU ARE GRATEFUL FOR — PEOPLE AND PETS

I truly hope you've experienced loving relationships with people in your life. However, after working with clients for twenty years, I understand that this isn't always the case. Perhaps there's someone from your past — a relative, teacher, coworker, or friend — who showed you kindness or helped you in some way. Or maybe you have people in your life right now, such as a partner or your children, who bring you joy. Sometimes, animals and pets make it easier to feel gratitude; they often become cherished family members, offering us unconditional love and always being happy to see us. Sinking into the love and gratitude you feel for a loved one — human or pet, whether still with us or passed on — can bring a warmth that touches your soul. You wouldn't be the person you are today without the people and animals who have come into your life and shared their love with you.

I taught a class where I asked people to recall a person they were grateful for in their life, past or present. I was saddened to have not just one, but two people tell me they could not think of one. I then extended this exercise to include pets or animals. Pets tend to give unconditional love and sometimes it is easier to tap into that love. You might not have had a person jumping up and down every time you arrived back home, but if you have had a dog, you have been lucky enough to experience this and feel the gratitude from them in every inch of your body.

PRACTICE:

Whether you have been fortunate enough to have a person in your life past or present that you felt love for and from, or whether it is easier to recall that feeling in connection with a pet — you have felt love from another being. Gratitude for that being connects you with them, no matter if they are around or not and can take you deeply into remembering the love you share(d).

While under the stream of water or as you wash, bring to mind a person or pet you are grateful for. Truly bring them in. Imagine their scent, how it felt to hold them close, and the sound of their voice or presence. If you like, recall a specific memory that made you feel grateful for them. Feel the love you shared and stay in that feeling for as long as you can. Say "thank you" to this person or pet for the love, kindness, peace, or whatever emotions they brought into your life. Feel their presence, soak in the gratitude, and if possible, feel their gratitude for you as well. Thank yourself for taking this time.

EXERCISE #5
GRATITUDE FOR NATURE

Whether it's the beach, the woods, flowers, trees, the sky, the moon and stars, the mountains, or watching a sunrise or sunset, I trust there's been a time — hopefully many — when nature brought you peace and filled you with awe. Nature's beauty and sounds — the wind, rain, bird calls, waves crashing on the shore, or even a storm — can be incredibly soothing. Some people even fall asleep to the sound of waves from a sound machine because it relaxes them so deeply.

Many people have favorite seasons: summer for its warmth and lushness, autumn for its vibrant colors, winter for its coolness and slower pace, or spring for its rebirth and flowering. Your connection to nature might differ from others', but what matters in this exercise is what brings you that deep sense of gratitude. Perhaps it's a specific place, like a summer beach house, a vacation spot, or even your own backyard.

For me, growing up in NYC, I found my sanctuary in Central Park. It was a space that offered peace and beauty amidst "the concrete jungle." I had to make a conscious effort to include nature in my life, and I invite you to do the same. No matter where you live, the opportunity exists to connect with nature in some way.

I had a client, "Nicole" who had so many negative experiences and trauma in her life, caused by people, that she had essentially written humanity off. Nicole had pets before, but as she was getting older, did not feel like adopting one and starting over. Her true love and connection became nature. Nicole had a very small yard but would keep herbs and plants inside her home and connect that way. Nicole didn't have the energy to be out for long, but she would drive to a park and sit on a bench and take in the natural environment around her. Nature was able to connect her with gratitude for this planet, even though she had a tough time here.

PRACTICE:

There are so many different ways to connect with nature, as Nicole demonstrated. You don't need to be sitting cross-legged on a mountaintop to take it all in. There are infinite ways for you to connect to the gratitude you experience for some aspect of Mother Nature, and there is great power in doing so. As Nicole aged, she got a few plants for outside her doorway and put a chair there, and that became the way she connected with nature. Get imaginative and know there is always a way you can connect, and it will be healing.

While under the stream of water or as you wash, bring to mind a place in nature, a moment spent in nature, or an aspect of nature you are grateful for. Engage all your senses — how does it feel, what smells are present, and what sounds can you hear? Visualize yourself in that natural setting and allow a smile to come to your face. Say "thank you" to Mother Nature, either out loud or to yourself, for the beauty and peace she provides. Stay in this moment for as long as it feels comfortable. The next time you do this exercise, try to extend that sense of connection and gratitude for even longer. Thank yourself for taking this time.

EXERCISE #6
GRATITUDE FOR TODAY

We've all heard the saying, "Tomorrow isn't promised." The truth is, none of us can truly know for sure what the next few days will bring. Mindfulness is about embracing the present moment. Practicing gratitude for today takes that concept a step deeper. It's about being mindful of what you are grateful for as you enter this day. You can focus on what you've already experienced — like your comfortable bed or the fact you are in a refreshing shower. Or you can focus on what you're looking forward to, such as lunch with a friend, a book you plan on reading today, or cooking a favorite meal. When we pause and express gratitude for today, we remind ourselves that life isn't as overwhelming as it might seem. This shift in perspective creates space for more goodness and even miracles to enter your life. Embracing gratitude is powerful, but practicing gratitude for *today* and the present moment? This can be truly life-changing.

When I was sick, I was repeating thoughts about everything I could NOT do that day — all the ways I did not feel good enough and was not going to be able to show up how I wanted. I was focused on the pain (which was attention-getting) and was busy beating myself up about my limitations. When I switched my mind to being grateful for things I was able to do *today*, things shifted. I focused on my ability to read to my kids in bed, even if I wasn't able to play with them the way I wanted. I appreciated that I had a comfy bed to lie in; that I was usually able to get to and from bed by myself; and the fact that often, while most of my body was in pain, my hands were not. And I was grateful that that I was able to have support with my kids, so I was not doing it alone. All of these were blessings I could sink into. By focusing on what was good today — I changed my tomorrow.

PRACTICE:

I know firsthand how easy it is to give into that human side of us that wants to turn to the negative — replaying things that are not as we want versus what we are grateful for. The beautiful news is we always have the ability to pay gratitude for *today*. We did wake up — that *alone* deserves gratitude. We get to breathe air, drink water, and we *get to choose* our thoughts.

While under the stream of water or as you wash, take a few deep breaths and bring yourself into the present moment. Think of something you're grateful for today. Once you have it in mind, dive deeper into why you are grateful for it. If possible, bring in every sense as you sink into this gratitude — *feel* that gratitude with every part of your being. Ask that gratitude be imbued into every cell of your being and bring a smile to your face. Stay in this feeling for as long as possible, at least for a few minutes. Please don't forget to thank yourself for taking the time to notice.

EXERCISE #7
GRATITUDE FOR SOMETHING YOU ARE LOOKING FORWARD TO

Looking forward to something adds excitement to life. It doesn't have to be anything big; maybe you have an exercise class this week, a walk after work, or lunch with a good friend on your schedule. Perhaps you've set aside some time for yourself, whether it's to dive into a book, engage in a hobby, or enjoy something else you love. You might also be looking forward to something a bit further in the future. Maybe you have planned a vacation, or there's a book, music or movie release that you're excited for. Perhaps you have scheduled a visit with a friend or family member, or booked a massage or another self-care treat. While tomorrow isn't guaranteed, having something to look forward to makes life more enjoyable. Think of the excitement a child feels as they await Christmas morning. The more we invite that childlike wonder into our lives, the more joy and excitement we experience.

I have found so many of my clients just living day to day on some kind of hamster wheel. There are many excuses I've heard for not planning something to look forward to — from being "too busy," to "having no money," to "not even knowing what would bring in joy because it has been so long." Only *you* can tap into what might bring you some joy or peace. But please, as you ask yourself what would excite you to anticipate, ask that annoying nay-saying voice to stand aside.

The simplest of steps can bring results. I had one client who got a library card and began taking out fictional books and reading a few minutes before bed. This brought her back to such a state of joy. She would look forward to bedtime every night with gratitude, as well as finishing the book and taking the next trip to the library where she could find another. This truly changed her life.

PRACTICE:

Whether you want to invite in something regular to look forward to, like my client did with her library trips and books, or you want to block time for something special for yourself — *any choice* is a gift to yourself. It allows you to let in some excitement and feel grateful and excited for the future.

Get comfortable and take a few deep breaths to center yourself. Set an intention to stay focused during the next few moments. While under the water or washing yourself, bring to mind something you're looking forward to. Allow yourself to feel the emotions that come with it. Is the emotion excitement, relief, peace, joy, a combination, or something else? Visualize yourself enjoying that activity, and thank yourself for setting aside time in the future for something you enjoy. Stay in this energy for as long as it feels good, or bring in other things you're excited about and repeat the process. As always, thank yourself for taking this time.

EXERCISE #8
GRATITUDE FOR YOUR WHOLE BODY

Our bodies perform incredible tasks every day, regulating our breath, blood, organs, and systems without any conscious effort on our part. Yet, we rarely acknowledge this, unless something goes wrong or starts to hurt. If we think about all our bodies have done for us so far (and how little gratitude we often show), it might resemble a one-sided, neglectful relationship.

We expect our bodies to function for us, and maybe we try to support them by eating somewhat well and getting some rest. We might even exercise somewhat regularly. But we can do much more to nurture and appreciate them. Our relationship with our bodies, and how we speak to and treat them, is crucial to our physical, mental, and emotional well-being. The shower is an ideal time to practice gratitude for your body — after all, you're already there, naked and vulnerable, in the perfect setting to connect with yourself.

I certainly gave my body so much grief when I was sick. I have also seen similar attitudes in most of my clients who faced chronic pain. After healing, I realized I was expecting what might be considered slave labor from my body, giving it no gratitude or positive energy and expecting it to work perfectly for me for nothing in return. I was eating okay and exercising when I could — didn't it *owe* me? I didn't say that, but in hindsight, it certainly felt like that was the energy I was putting out there.

PRACTICE:

If you are like me, you might not have ever thought of giving yourself gratitude for your body. I have even had clients write love letters to their bodies. Today is a new day, and it can begin now and only take a few moments. You might be surprised how quickly you feel results when you start sending positive energy and gratitude to your beautiful body!!

Start by scanning your body from head to toe, offering thanks to each part, either out loud or in your mind. Begin with your head, and move down through your face, neck, shoulders, arms, fingers, and so on, all the way to your feet and toes. As you focus on each part, feel gratitude for the ways it has supported you. Alternatively, you can express gratitude as you wash each part of your body, saying a small "thank you" with each touch. This combination of touch and gratitude can make the experience even more powerful. If possible, really feel into the gratitude for each part of your body. You might even elaborate — thank your eyes and nose for allowing you to see and smell, for example. Notice how your body feels when you're finished. Thank yourself for taking this time.

EXERCISE #9
GRATITUDE FOR A SPECIFIC PART OF YOUR BODY

We often only focus on specific parts of our bodies when they hurt. When we get headaches, our attention shifts to our head. If our stomach aches, we zero in on that discomfort. During my seven years of chronic pain, much of the pain was concentrated in my legs, and I spent a lot of time fixated on that pain. Pain is distracting and demanding of attention — I know this well. But I also learned that focusing on pain amplifies it, sending more energy to the area, which can intensify the discomfort.

When I began to shift my focus and express gratitude for my legs — remembering how many years they allowed me to walk and dance — they began to feel better. Think about how you would respond to a loved one or pet in pain. Would you offer them love and gratitude, or would you react with anger and frustration? How would they respond to these emotions? Showing love and gratitude to parts of your body that have received "less-than-positive attention" can transform the energy, sometimes very quickly.

PRACTICE:

What part of your body have you literally "blamed" or "beat up" because it was causing you pain, just as I did with my legs? Whatever part comes to mind first is the one best for this exercise. You can work your way through different parts of yourself on different days. It is best to focus on *one* body part for this exercise to truly feel this shift.

Stand under the stream of water and focus on the part of your body that has been giving you a challenge, or gently wash this body part while saying "thank you." Reflect on the years this part of your body has worked for you. Generate feelings of compassion and love, as you would for a loved one in pain, and direct those feelings toward this part of your body. If it feels right, tell that body part you love it and are grateful for it, either silently or out loud. Stay in this space for as long as feels comfortable. If there are other parts of your body that could use some love and gratitude, extend this practice to them as well. Thank yourself for taking this time.

Chapter 2
Water – Beautiful, Healing Water
Exercises and Practices (10-15)

We are made up of mostly water — about 60 percent —with some parts of our body, like the brain, consisting of up to 95 percent water. Water is a miraculous element with incredible healing properties. Astrologically, water is associated with intuition and emotions. In shamanic traditions, water represents growth and nourishment for all beings on the planet. Spiritually, water is associated with intuition, innovation, and change. Water can also be associated with wisdom, as in the Taoist image of water always finding its way around obstacles. Water is seen as a life giver in Buddhism, where it symbolizes purity, calmness and clarity. Many people have reported gaining insights while in or around water. No matter what symbolism you take from it, water is deeply healing and transformative and deserves a ton of gratitude.

Masaru Emoto's work with water was truly groundbreaking. He demonstrated that human thoughts and words have a profound effect on water. When frozen, water crystals formed in response to positive thoughts or words appear beautiful, while those formed in response to negative thoughts and words appear distorted or unattractive. As a bonus exercise, you might want to write a kind and loving word on the outside of your water bottle or dispenser — it makes a difference!!

I have had some of my most amazing realizations and inspirations in the shower or bathtub. It truly is a place of magic, when you tune into it and allow your mind to take a little bit of a break from the noise of the outside world.

Given the power of water, and since you are in the shower during these mindfulness exercises, it makes sense to tap into this powerful element. This chapter explores different ways to harness the transformative energy of water.

EXERCISE #10
GRATITUDE FOR WATER

Continuing with the theme of gratitude, there is great power in acknowledging the ways water has brought joy and sustenance to your life.

Why are you grateful for water? What associations do you have with it? Maybe you are good at staying hydrated and know the refreshing feeling of a cold glass of water after a workout or on a hot day. Maybe you are an avid coffee or tea drinker and appreciate how water makes that drink possible! Perhaps you love swimming and have fond memories of it throughout your life, or enjoy a relaxing soak in a hot tub. Maybe you find peace sitting by the water — whether it's the beach, a stream, the ocean, or a lake. You might be fascinated by the creatures that live in water, like fish, dolphins, or whales. Or perhaps you are amazed at how much of your body is made up of water.

I often recommend clients get near water or listen to the sound of water. There is something about watching the way water moves around rocks, never stopping, simply flowing, that is calming. Listening to water (minus the having to get up and pee part) is also very calming. If you have a busy mind, water sounds can be wonderful to put on a noise machine or app, including as you are falling asleep.

Since you've picked up this book, you probably enjoy a

good shower or bath and appreciate the many qualities water offers whether or not you have been conscious of them up until this point.

PRACTICE:

There are so many reasons to be grateful for water. Only you know the reasons that particularly resonate with you. It can be as simple as you have running water to clean yourself with! There are many people that do *not* have that luxury.

As you watch the water flow from the showerhead, give thanks for it. As it touches your body, express gratitude. Bring to mind a few ways you are thankful for water and replay those thoughts as you stand under the stream. Say "thank you" to the water, and if you feel moved, you can elaborate: "Thank you, water, for bringing me cleanliness. Thank you for your healing properties. I love you, water." There is no right or wrong way to do this. Enter the shower with water on your mind and a heart full of gratitude. Let your appreciation flow as the water touches your skin. Thank yourself for taking this time.

EXERCISE #11
HEAD AND SHOULDERS EXERCISE

Our brain is an incredible organ that holds our memories, manages our bodily systems, and harmonizes the logical left side with the more intuitive right side. It houses our scalp and most of our senses — sight, smell, taste, hearing — and our face, which makes us uniquely ourselves. Our head also holds our thoughts, which can often run wild.

You have probably heard the expression "carrying the weight of the world on your shoulders." It's true — stress can cause tension that draws our shoulders up around our necks. But you can feel that stress melt away when you intentionally breathe and release your shoulders. The head and shoulders are two amazing parts of the body to focus on as you wash away stress and tension.

I often find my shoulders clenched up or slightly forward. I shouldn't be surprised by now, but I *am* each time I sit down to meditate. I begin my daily meditation by noticing my breath and "relaxing my body," part by part. When I get to my shoulders, there they are again, "hangin' out" way higher on my body or pushed forward — definitely not in the most relaxed state. I've done this work for 20 years and still carry some stress in my shoulders. Okay, noted; I will keep working on it, grateful I do have the awareness to return them to a state of deep peace and relaxation.

PRACTICE:

It might be fun to take note of where your shoulders are during the day. If you work at a desk, do they tend to feel tight or are they hunched forward? Do you sometimes get tension or stress headaches? By tuning into these two parts of your body, you better equip yourself with the ability to notice and to return to a deep sense of peace and relaxation!

When you're ready for this practice, place yourself so that your head is under the stream of water in the shower. As the water hits your head, take a moment to give thanks for your brain, your eyes, ears, nose, mouth, and senses. Feel the water flowing over your scalp and imagine it washing away your thoughts, relaxing you more deeply. Stay in this soothing sensation for as long as it feels good. When you're ready, shift your focus to your shoulders. Position yourself so the water cascades over them, and as you do, ask your shoulders to relax even more. Thank the water for helping your shoulders release tension and drop away from your neck. Picture them sinking lower and relaxing further as the water beats down on them. Stay here, giving gratitude to the water and your shoulders, for as long as it feels comfortable. Thank yourself for taking this time.

EXERCISE #12
WATER STREAM OF CONSCIOUSNESS

Each stream of water holds blessings for us, but often we stand under the shower without paying much attention. What if we used each stream as a moment for gratitude? I love this practice because it is always different. As I stand under the water, I watch the streams pour down and imagine what each one means. One stream might represent abundance flowing into my life, while another brings calm. If your showerhead adjusts, play around with it — the different jet streams can make visualizing even easier.

Most of us have had a conversation where we truly could not remember how we got from one topic all the way to another. Sometimes we've even had something we deeply wanted to communicate to someone but got so caught up in the current topics, we forgot our original stream of thought. This often happens when I speak with my grown kids, so I have taken to writing down topics I need to speak about with them. We can get so caught up in catching up that the matters that felt "important" are forgotten. Similarly, we can get caught up in the routine of another shower without taking that time to truly appreciate those streams of water that are cleaning us and bringing in energy.

There is power in noticing and creating the intention that this *is* important and where we want to focus.

PRACTICE:

Water and the power of the shower offer us a time to focus all our attention on what we want to bring in. Maybe you are looking for more health, better routines, more abundance, or closer friendships. When you focus on what you want and picture it literally "pouring into" your life, you send out that welcoming energy, and it feels really good to claim it and know you are worthy of it!

Adjust your showerhead to a setting that feels best for you. Position yourself under the water so you can see the streams or hold out your hands to "catch" them. Visualize what each stream represents: perhaps abundance, health, or peace. You might say, "Thank you for showering me with health," and feel the stream hitting your body. This practice allows you to be mindful, playful, and intentional — infusing your life with what you desire. Don't forget to thank the water for its magic and yourself for taking this time!

EXERCISE #13
WATER TAKING STRESS AND PAIN DOWN THE DRAIN

This exercise uses visualization to release stress or pain. You can literally imagine the water washing away your stress or pain, and see it disappearing down the drain. Whether you're starting or ending your day, mentally tell yourself you are letting go, and allow the water to do the work. This can be especially powerful for physical pain — visualize the water locating and removing it from your body.

I've had clients become dedicated to this exercise and use it daily. This is an easy one and can be so invigorating. I had a client, "Lucy," who had a very stressful relationship with her mother. Every time she got back from visiting her mother, Lucy would take a shower and witness that stress disappearing. Lucy said it changed the way she felt about her mom. Since she knew she would be able to release the stress after seeing her mom, she would show up for their visits in a very different energy state. Her mom felt Lucy's energy shift, and their relationship was able to improve and become a little less stressful for both of them!

PRACTICE:

Maybe there is a situation you face each day that stresses you out or a part of your body that feels and holds stress. Is there a relationship like the one Lucy had with her mom that came to mind when you read about her?

Decide what you want to let go of — stress, pain, or both. As the water touches your body, say, "Thank you for removing my stress/pain." Watch the water as it goes down the drain and feel the relief. As fresh water continues to flow, thank it for filling you with renewed energy. Repeat this as many times as needed, feeling the release and giving gratitude for the water's healing power. Thank yourself for taking this time.

EXERCISE #14
VISCERALLY NAMING HOW WATER MAKES YOU FEEL

Often in the shower, our minds wander, and we become unaware of what we're doing. I know there were days I was so distracted that I had a hard time remembering if I had already washed my hair or not! Water is a healing element that deserves our attention. By tuning into how it feels on your body, you can bring yourself back to the present moment and connect with the sensations water evokes. Connecting with our senses is a powerful way to reset and be present. Focusing on how water makes you feel deepens this and invites in the healing element of water.

Many times the shower is a time when we tend to focus on what's next rather than the joy and gratitude of receiving this element. I love this exercise as it is a very quick way to kind of shake myself and tell myself, "Hey there, pay attention please — this is for you." We are so blessed to have running water and to be able to utilize a shower; naming how the water makes us feel is an even deeper way of connecting with its magic.

PRACTICE:

This is super powerful since you are connecting with your body and the water and appreciating their connection with each other. It's about as easy as it gets and is a way to bring yourself back to the power in the present moment and your thoughts and sensations in the now.

As the water hits different parts of your body, name how it makes you feel. For example: "The water feels relaxing on my head," or "It feels warm on my belly." You may be surprised by the range of sensations and emotions that arise when you are truly present with water. If you feel inclined, thank the water for the sensations it allows you to experience. You can incorporate this practice daily to stay mindful and present during your shower. Thank yourself for taking this time.

EXERCISE #15
WASHING AWAY LIMITING THOUGHTS

This exercise is inspired by my experience and a story I wrote that was included in Neale Donald Walsch's book, *GodTalk: Experiences of Humanity's Connections with a Higher Power*.

In the story, called "The Supernatural Washing Machine," I visualized limiting words on shirts and washed them clean in a supernatural washing machine. I've adapted this for the shower. Water can help you release limiting beliefs, much like cleansing dirty laundry.

Oh boy, we've all heard them. Whether it be from a family member, teacher, partner, friend, co-worker, or someone else in our lives, we've all received a negative comment that prompted *just* enough doubt within us to have it "stick." My step-grandmother always loved to tell me when it looked like I "put on a few pounds." I've had clients tell me of horrific things their parents have said to them, some as extreme as wishing they were never born. These words eat into our subconscious mind and if not looked at, become our inner dialogue. I say — let's wash that nonsense away!

PRACTICE:

Limiting thoughts or beliefs usually come from someone else, but you may have been replaying them in your mind for so long that they feel like part of you. These limitations can look like doubts about your physical, mental, emotional, or financial wellness.

Before starting, identify one or two limiting beliefs you've been telling yourself, (e.g., "I'm not good enough"). As you stand under the water, close your eyes and imagine holding a t-shirt with one of those limiting beliefs written on it. Place the shirt under the water and visualize the words washing away, disappearing down the drain. Imagine yourself wringing out the shirt and hanging it up, now clean and free of those limiting beliefs. Repeat with other limiting thoughts as needed, feeling the release each time. Thank yourself and the water for helping to cleanse these negative beliefs.

Chapter 3
Using Water to Help Feel Empowered

(Exercises 16–21)

Water is a powerful element, and as we have noted, it makes up the majority of our bodies. Research, such as Masaru Emoto's work on water crystals, shows that water can change its structure in response to emotions and intentions. By tapping into your emotions, intentions, affirmations, and mantras, you can use water to feel more empowered.

My life changed, as did the lives of many of my clients, when we began to change our inner dialogue and tap into our emotions. It's easy to be on autopilot and easier than ever these days with the countless distractions of technology. But the shower can be one time when you choose to notice 1) how you are feeling 2) how you want to feel and 3) choose dialogue that matches the intention. These exercises all help deeply with that change and only take a few minutes that you already have. They are powerful on their own but become even more potent in the shower. You can also try them in front of a mirror, either before or after your shower. There's no wrong way to do this. Experiment and find what works best for you.

EXERCISE #16
EMOTIONS

Emotions are our guideposts, but we often don't fully acknowledge them. Instead of just recognizing extreme emotions like happiness or anger, it's important to identify the many other emotions we feel. The more accurately we name our emotions, the more power we gain over them, allowing us to respond mindfully instead of reacting impulsively.

Rumi's poem, "The Guest House," beautifully illustrates why emotions are important.

> This being human is a guest house.
> Every morning a new arrival.
> A joy, a depression, a meanness,
> some momentary awareness comes
> as an unexpected visitor.
> Welcome and entertain them all!
> Even if they're a crowd of sorrows,
> who violently sweep your house
> empty of its furniture,
> still, treat each guest honorably.
> He may be clearing you out
> for some new delight.
> The dark thought, the shame, the malice,
> meet them at the door laughing,

and invite them in.
Be grateful for whoever comes,
because each has been sent
as a guide from beyond.

—Rumi, The Guest House

As I've noticed in my work with clients and with my own experience, we usually name the most common, broadly defined emotions when asked how we feel, such as happiness or sadness. Doing so does not allow us to get to the "root" of the matter and process our feelings.

Brené Brown's work in "*The Atlas of the Heart: Mapping Meaningful Connection and the Language of Human Experience*" shines a light on the vast array of human emotions and how important it is to focus on which specific emotions we are truly experiencing. Watching Brown's program based on this book brought me a ton of tears and deep healing. If we say we are "sad," we may be feeling grief, loneliness, disappointment, or some other emotion. If you say each of these words out loud, you may notice they bring up very different feelings.

I often ask my clients to expand on what they are feeling to get to the real emotion that has emerged. Often, even in naming the true and root emotion, you can begin to find some inner compassion and healing.

I have come up with the following method to nurture emotions, and I highly recommend you try this a few times at least to get the hang of it.

PRACTICE:

Remember, the more you zero in on the exact emotion you are feeling, the easier it is to process it and move the heck on!!

While in the shower, close your eyes (if comfortable) and place your hand(s) over your heart. Ask yourself:

1. How do I truly feel right now? Dive deeper than general emotions like "happy" or "sad" to identify the root emotion

2. What emotion can I bring in to support this feeling? For example, if you feel overwhelmed, you might bring in inner peace. Name the supporting emotion.

3. Recall a time when you felt this supportive emotion. Visualize every detail: how it felt in your body, and any scents, sounds, or visuals associated with that moment. Reconnect with that emotion and bask in it.

4. Thank yourself for taking the time to notice and nurture your emotions.

EXERCISE #17
AFFIRMATIONS — TELL YOURSELF WHAT YOU WANT AND ARE READY FOR!

Affirmations can be a powerful way to focus your thoughts and energy on what you want to bring into your life. I believe affirmations work best when they mostly align with your beliefs and what you feel is true but also invite in more of what you are ready for. For example, when I was working on healing from chronic illness, I used affirmations like, "I am working on getting better every day," which felt achievable yet empowering. If I would have told myself "I am healed," my body would have called BS, as I was still in so much pain, daily. Please make sure the affirmations you choose resonate with you.

I have found that when you use affirmations that are far from your current reality, they can create more resistance than positive change. For example, if you are struggling to pay bills but are saying, "I am a billionaire" every day, your subconscious will sense the gap and it might actually bring up negative emotions and energy. A more aligned affirmation might be, "I am inviting in more wealth" or "I am abundant." Recognizing the abundance you already have — whether in health, love, food, or other areas — helps to invite more abundance into your finances as well.

Aim for affirmations that are mostly true for you and feel aligned but are also inviting in what you want for your life, for the best results. *I am* statements are particularly powerful; declare what you are, or what you are ready to achieve for optimal impact. The *most* powerful affirmation I have heard of *that works wonders* begins, "I am so happy and grateful now that ...". Insert what you are already grateful for in your life here or what you are looking to manifest. For example, "I am so happy and grateful now that money comes into my life in many different ways." Or "I am so happy and grateful now that my health is improving every day." Try a few out and see how they feel.

PRACTICE:

Knowing what you want is the first step to creating the perfect affirmation for you. Please make it easy to remember. Remember the power of the "I am" statements as well as the affirmations beginning "I am so happy and grateful now that …". Above all — have *fun* creating these affirming statements. Become childlike and *feel* them when you say them, inviting in that new energy!

While in the shower, choose an affirmation that feels right for you. As you say it, really feel it. For example, if your affirmation is, "Everything always works out for me," think of an example when something did work out in your favor. The more emotion you bring into the affirmation, the more powerful it becomes. Repeat for at least 30 seconds or as long as you feel comfortable. You may choose to alternate between a few affirmations. This is your practice, so make it your own. Thank yourself for taking this time.

EXERCISE #18
DAILY INTENTIONS — WHAT DO YOU WANT TO CREATE TODAY?

Intentions are like a plan for what you want to bring into your life. Often, we focus on what we don't want, but setting clear intentions helps us shift our energy toward what we do want. Setting a daily intention helps bring focus and positivity to your day. Instead of being caught up in your to-do list or what you're dreading, choose what you want to bring into your day — whether it's laughter, abundance, joy, peace, or a pleasant surprise.

This is such a fun one! It also allows you to see how much you *do*, in fact, contribute to creating your reality. I've had clients begin with things like, "I am going to find the perfect parking spot today." Or "I am calling in something funny." Choose something that is tangible, so that afterward you can say, "Whoa, it is so cool that happened." It's great to start off with things that might seem inconsequential or "small," then work up to the ones that feel bigger. Sometimes we need some *proof* before we can let the bigger ones in.

I had a client, "Lily," who was a single mom of three young children and never had time for herself. Lily had no family or close friends living close by, as she had moved for her husband's job and then her husband left. Lily's intention for a few days in a row was to be able to gain time for herself, although she had no clue how that would manifest. After a couple of days of intending this outcome, an old friend she hadn't seen for a while came for a visit and volunteered to watch the kids for her while she had a staycation day of relaxation. Lily took a bath, read and pampered herself for three whole hours. (That feels like days when you have not had it in a while!). Lily could go back to parenting with a smile and was amazed her intention had become a reality! As a bonus, her friend loved the time with the kids so much that she promised to come back once a month to help Lily out!

PRACTICE:

What do you need more of or want evidence of in your life? Some time alone? A bout of laughter? If it is something "small," trust that it will happen soon. If it is a bigger ask, you might want to try this practice a few days in a row as Lily did and see what happens!

While in the shower, think about what you want to call into your day. Maybe you need more peace, laughter, or a pleasant surprise. Create a sentence or a few words that reflect your intention and repeat them to yourself. So perhaps you say to yourself, "I am inviting in more peace today." Or "I intend to laugh more today." Smile, feel the water, and remember a time when you felt the emotion you're calling in. Thank yourself for taking this moment to set your intention for the day.

EXERCISE #19
INTENTIONS – WHAT DO YOU WANT TO CREATE?
(LONG TERM)

Contemplating and setting intentions on what we want for the long term can excite and propel us forward. Whether you want to manifest healthier relationships, financial abundance, or a regular meditation practice, intentions put that energy into motion. This is about setting goals and getting clear on what you are ready for and working toward. Intentions are also an act of self-love — telling yourself you are ready and worthy of more.

When I have come up with clear intentions, I truly have been able to manifest what some might call "miracles" in my life: a book deal with my desired publisher, the love of my life, a home, and so much more. I have helped hundreds of other people do the same. One of my favorite experiences was with a client, "Mary." She was in the same job for ten years, and while she had moved up the ranks, she felt like she had hit a glass ceiling, with the men holding the key roles in her corporation. She felt under-valued. We worked together to guide her to set the intention of really being seen in her job, valued and offered her "dream job" within the organization. She was amazed that within one month of doing this work with intentions, she received many accolades and the offer for her dream job with a higher salary than she had ever imagined. This stuff works!! You have to know what you want to call it in, and Mary's example and my own life examples are *just* the beginning!

PRACTICE:

Like Mary, you may be surprised at what happens when you begin to apply this attention to intention. Often, we walk around dwelling on what we don't want or don't like. When we switch to what we are intending to call in, be it for the short or long term, and when we stick with it, it causes change. As with the daily intentions, start with something that doesn't mean so much to you to see very quick results. Then, work your way to the bigger and more important things in your life. Prepare to be amazed and welcome in change!!

Think about whether you want to focus on a short-term or long-term intention and choose an area of your life to work on. Create a clear, concise statement that embodies this intention. While standing under the water, say your intention and imagine how you will feel when it becomes reality. These can be things like, "I intend to have healthy relationships in my life," or "I intend to create a solid business for myself." Allow yourself to bask in the emotions you will feel when that intention becomes reality, while the water enhances your visualization. Thank yourself for this awareness. During this time, you can also ask for guidance or a step you may need to take to make your intention a reality. If you feel guided, set a few intentions for different areas of your life. Please thank yourself for taking this time.

EXERCISE #20
A MANTRA FOR YOUR DAY

A mantra is a word or sound that is repeated to help focus the mind and bring about a sense of calm and concentration. It serves as an anchor for the mind, while also helping to calm the body and reduce stress. Mantras can also have ancient origins, carrying specific meanings and vibrations. One of the most well-known mantras is "Om," which in Hinduism is believed to be the original vibration of the universe — the sound from which all others emerge.

The vagus nerve, a crucial part of the body's nervous system, plays a key role in calming us down. Practices like humming activate the vagus nerve and can lead to deep relaxation. It is also said that simply thinking of these sounds repeatedly can have healing and calming effects on the mind and body.

To begin this exercise, choose a sound or word that resonates with you. Here are a few suggestions to get you started, but feel free to improvise or create your own:

- Repeat the sound "Om."
- Repeat the word "Peace."
- Repeat the word "Love."
- Repeat the sound "HU." (Pronounced HEW)
- Repeat the word "Joy."

These are just examples, and there are countless mantras you can explore. I encourage you to research and find one that truly aligns with how you want to feel. The key is to remain mindful while repeating your chosen mantra.

These mantras all have serious power as will *any* that you find resonate and take the time to repeat.

I'd like to share my experience with the mantra "HU" (pronounced "Hew"). I had heard of the sound before, but it came up again in a major way in my life a few months ago. I knew that in ancient Egypt, HU was considered the first word uttered — the word of creation. I also had heard that HU was an ancient word for God or "The Voice of God." Through synchronicities, I found the word/sound HU again, which is the key component of the spiritual group Eckankar. They believe that chanting HU takes you deeper inside yourself and also connects you with God/the Universe. There are many instances they cite of "miracles" happening when chanting this ancient sound. I downloaded the app where there are thousands of people chanting this sound, and I had a pretty profound experience. I encourage you to check it out if the idea appeals to you. It is always about what resonates with you and having some fun exploring.

PRACTICE:

Did the story of HU interest you? If so begin there! If not, choose another one I mentioned or a word that comes to mind when you think of "mantra."

Before you step into the shower, decide on the mantra you will focus on for that day. As the water flows over you, begin repeating your mantra. Don't just recite the word or sound — really immerse yourself in it. Feel its resonance in your body. If possible, repeat your mantra for a few minutes.

Saying or speaking the mantra out loud is ideal, as the vibration of your voice can enhance its effect. However, if you feel more comfortable repeating it silently in your mind, that is perfectly fine as well. Whether repeating it out loud or silently, both have huge benefits and connect you with the present moment. Continue repeating your mantra for as long as you can stay mindful.

When you are done, take a deep breath, absorbing the resonance of the mantra, and exhale any lingering stress. Finally, thank yourself for taking this time to choose a mantra and repeat it, acknowledging the intention and care you've given to this practice.

EXERCISE #21
HAVENING

Havening is a powerful technique that can help alleviate anxiety and promote deep relaxation. In this book, we focus on havening as a distinctive self-soothing motion, where you cross your arms and gently stroke from your shoulders down to your elbows. This simple yet effective movement resets your nervous system, sending a signal to your body that you are safe. In just a few moments, this can bring a sense of relief and well-being. Some people also find it helpful to say to themselves, "I am safe," while performing the motion, but the action alone can have a profound effect.

The beauty of this technique is that it can be practiced anywhere — in the shower, at work, on the couch — anytime you need to regain a sense of calm. For the purpose of this book, the exercise is intended to be done in the shower, but know that it is a versatile tool you can use whenever you feel out of sorts. After just a few moments of practicing havening, you may find yourself feeling more relaxed, safe, and ready to start your day with a sense of empowerment.

I had a client, "Matt," who always felt anxious. Matt had a very rough upbringing and was still suffering from the effects of never truly feeling love on a deep level. We were on a video call when he first tried this exercise. After two minutes, he started to cry huge tears of relief. It felt like he was giving himself the love and comfort that he had looked for all of this life. Matt started practicing havening not just in the shower, but when he woke up, anytime he felt anxious, and before bed. He said that within one week he felt more relaxed than he had in all of his 35 years. This is an easy and accessible technique that can bring in such relief and peace.

PRACTICE:

Whether you have felt a sense of deep anxiousness like Matt, or just have times of feeling uneasy, the havening technique works. We all deserve that calm and loving touch and reassurance. Havening gives you the ability to grant that comfort to yourself.

While in the shower, find a comfortable position that feels right for you. Personally, I like to have the water running down my back while I practice this technique, but the most important thing is for you to feel at ease. Whether you choose to close your eyes or keep them open, focus on creating a safe and nurturing environment for yourself.

When you're ready, gently fold your arms across your chest. Slowly and lightly stroke from your shoulders down to your elbows on both arms simultaneously. Move as slowly as possible, allowing yourself to savor the sensation. If it feels right, you can also repeat the words, "I am safe," as you continue the gentle stroking motion.

Take your time with this, practicing for a few minutes, and notice how much more relaxed you feel afterward.

Once you've completed the exercise, take a moment to thank yourself for dedicating this time to your well-being. Remember that this soothing technique can be done anywhere and anytime, whenever you need to invite peace and safety into your life.

Chapter 4
Ways to Adapt These Exercises for the Bathtub and Life

Notes on the Book and Your Continued Mindfulness Practice

Above all, *please* have fun with this journey. Make it a game of sorts with yourself. If you take it too seriously, the human tendency will be to find it "hard" and to give up. Mindfulness is a choice in every moment. I like to challenge myself and ask myself at the end of the day, "How much of the day was spent mindfully, and how much was run on autopilot?"

When I am with clients, I am 100 percent mindful. When I am meditating or doing any of my spiritual practices, I am 100 percent mindful. And of course by now, the shower is my dedicated mindfulness time. (Okay, 90 percent of the time it is!). But it is interesting to me to see how many times I might have started to worry or to go down a rabbit hole during my mindfulness time in the shower. I *teach* this stuff and know it is very easy to get pulled into some old pattern of thought. Be *gentle* and kind with yourself in this process.

I find myself chuckling or rolling my eyes at myself often. It's okay to find this whole "being human" thing rather funny, but it's not okay to beat yourself up every time you find yourself in a pattern you are not too happy with. That fuels disempowerment and discourages creating the new habit of mindfulness.

It's a journey, not a race. Any time you catch yourself and bring yourself back to the present moment is a huge *win*. Pat yourself on the back and recognize you are making progress and are heading toward being the best version of you. You could not ask for anything more!

Ways to Adapt These Exercises for the Bathtub

Some people take baths instead of showering. You can use these exercises anywhere and adapt them. Instead of feeling the stream of water on you, place your hands in and out of the water or "play" with the water in some other way. I am never one to say, "You *need* to do things my way, or else." This is about *you* becoming aware of your thoughts and coming up with easy and *fun* ways to become more mindful.

You can also increase the effectiveness of these exercises in the bathtub by investing in essential oils and Epsom salts. Smell is a powerful sense and can also help you sink deeper into mindfulness and get out of your brain and the endless loop it likes to repeat. My favorite essential oils are Sahu Oils.

Ways to Adapt These Exercises into Daily Life

Most of these exercises can be adapted to use in your everyday life. Gratitude is a quick go-to when you're looking to change up your energy. You can even set alarms on your phone for a few times through your day as a "check-in." When the alarm sounds, you can then notice where your mind was just before, and consider whether a few moments of being still and/or utilizing a mindfulness exercise would provide benefit.

Remember those 60,000 thoughts a day? The number sounds overwhelming, but know that *you* can have control over most of them with your intention and attention. The more mindful you are, the more your life can shift in beautiful and seemingly miraculous ways. We cannot create new from old programming.

I mentioned early on in this book that the *most* powerful times of day are when you are falling asleep and when you are waking up. At those times, your subconscious is more tuned in and your thoughts go deeper. If you can incorporate these mindfulness exercises at the beginning and end of your day, in addition to your shower time, you will be inviting in a lot more peace into your life. Remember most of these exercises take minutes!

Please thank yourself for any time you bring yourself back to the current moment and CHOOSE mindfulness!

ACKNOWLEDGEMENTS

I am deeply grateful to Ditte Young for writing the foreword to this book. I first discovered Ditte through the life-changing podcast *The Telepathy Tapes*, and from the very beginning, there was a profound resonance. When I later watched her TED Talk, that connection only deepened.

Ditte is a true kindred spirit. Her work in animal communication and telepathy is not only powerful—it's a luminous reminder of the unseen threads that connect us all. She embodies the quiet strength it takes to truly *listen* beyond words, which made her the perfect person to introduce this book.

Her presence radiates kindness, love, and authenticity, and the way she shares her gifts is a heart-offering to a world that needs more of exactly that. I am honored and humbled by her contribution.

I could not have written this book without the support of my husband, Vinny. He is my best friend, biggest supporter, and cheerleader, making life flow and more joyful in ways I never knew possible. I also want to thank my kids and Vinny's kids: Alex, Carter, Alissa, and Cassondra, who are now grown and continue to inspire me. It hasn't been easy growing up in today's world, but they each shine in their own way, have found amazing partners, and have grown into authentic, brilliant adults whom I admire deeply.

My mom was my first and constant source of inspiration. Her passing was the catalyst that allowed me to begin and sustain my own daily meditation and mindfulness practice. It's been over four years of a steady practice. I miss our daily calls, but I feel her love and support every day. I wouldn't be who I am today without her, and I am deeply grateful for the 50 years I had with her on this planet. My stepdad, Whitney, was with my mom for 35 years and also had his influence. Whitney meditated and wrote every single day, had a degree in religion, and was highly intelligent. Whitney was also extremely generous, expressing admiration for how I got things done, and always offering me praise and support. I was fortunate that both my parents were writers and encouraged me to write from a young age. My dad taught me how to read when I was two, which fueled my love of learning and the written word. I am grateful for the support.

I also want to express my gratitude to my friends and colleagues, who have been a constant source of support, cheering me and this book on: Seana, Cheryl, Marguerite, Enolia, Efrat, Jim, Mindy, and my mentor, Justine. They all encouraged me to write this down and keep going, emphasizing the importance of sharing these practices so others can experience the power and ease of bringing mindfulness into their daily lives. I have referenced some of these amazing people and their work in the Resources section in the back of this book.

I am also blessed to have many lifelong friends (for at least four decades), who have all shaped who I am.

- **Veronica**: Our moms were best friends since they were in 4th grade, so I have known her since her birth, a year after my own. Every talk we have offers inspiration.
- **Hillary**: I've known her since I was nine, and we grew up together, navigating NYC, sharing a lot of stoop-sitting and celebrating our birthdays.
- **Julie**: We've known each since age twelve and have shared so many similar interests — games, hiking, summer road trips, visits to both parents' country houses, and more.
- **Mindy**: I have known her since my sleep-away camp days. We went decades not being in touch, but when we reconnected, it felt like not a day had passed.

I also want to thank my friends who walk with me, listen to me, and make me laugh and think: Leslie, Janis, Teri, Jen.

- I am always grateful to my friend Angela for the critical part she played in my physical healing.
- I am grateful to Amy for her belief in me and my gifts and for being on this wild spiritual journey with me for over a decade!

I am also deeply grateful for every teacher, mentor and class I have taken. As well as the brilliant authors I have read on this journey. I am a lifelong student and would not be exactly where I am without each teaching. I know I am blessed to have so much love in my life. It is being around such inspirational and loving people and material that enables me to stay excited and inspired, and to stand in love and awe.

I also need to thank the TSPA team and my editor, Kathie. I tried the published author route and the self-publishing route all by myself. Both had their advantages but both also felt like something was missing. Having a team that believed in me and my book, with the knowledge to help me on my journey, has been priceless. It is the way I see moving forward with all my books in the future and for that, I am forever grateful. Thank you Megan, Kathie, Ira, my designer Ashley, and the whole TSPA team!! You were the most perfect delivery team for my book, baby!! I am forever grateful!

I feel such deep gratitude for those who took some time to review my book, give me feedback and write reviews. This book had my heart since it was a concept, and to see it be born and have people receive it is something I feel such deep gratitude for.

Lastly but not least, I want to thank my clients, and other friends, family members, and colleagues in my life. I have learned from each interaction and have grown from each conversation. Even the more challenging experiences, and sometimes *especially* the more challenging experiences, allowed me to tap into strength I did not know I had.

RESOURCES

I am blessed to have people around me who support, love and encourage me on my journey. They are both close friends and colleagues who truly want the best for me and this planet.

I have been constantly inspired by them and their work in this world, so I want to share them with you — trusting that tapping into their wisdom can assist you in your mindfulness journey.

CHERYL DEDECKER

Cheryl is a very gifted hypnotist. I have known her for years, and she has been a source of support through my mom's sickness and her passing, and she has helped me more than I can say. Her love of helping others shines through. We have led workshops together and share our love of board games, good food, and so much more. I am blessed to call her a good friend. I know first-hand how hypnotism can help the mind. Cheryl is gifted at leading hypnosis sessions and also teaching self-hypnosis, so you can use it as a tool moving forward.

Biography

Cheryl DeDecker (M.S., BCH, Oneonta, NY) has a Master's Degree in Counseling Psychology and is a National Guild of Hypnotists (NGH) Board Certified Hypnotist. She spent

20 years as a licensed Professional Counselor, utilizing Cognitive Behavioral Therapy and specializing in Women's Health and Stress Management. She has specialized hypnosis certifications in Complementary Medical Hypnosis, Hypno-Fertility, and HypnoCoaching®.

Cheryl is also trained as a Tai Chi Easy Leader and a Heart Rhythms drum circle facilitator. Cheryl loves her work as a "brain coach", empowering clients to lead their best lives through learning effective tools for change. If you would like to learn more about her sleep program or any of her services, please visit her site, Compass Coaching. cherylscompass.com

DITTE YOUNG

Ditte is a certified family therapist specialized in helping children who suffer from autism, brain damage, OCD, eating disorders, anxiety, depressions and so much more. Besides helping families in therapy, Ditte is also the mother of her autistic son Philip. He was born blind, has autism and minor brain damage as well. Ditte has helped him develop his eyesight making him capable of using a tablet, watch TV and read with enlarged letters. Ditte shares the many tools and gifts she had as a professional and mother to families in need of help. Website: ditteyoung.net

EFRAT SHOKEF

Efrat and I met via my shamanic teacher, and we were all in a writing group together. Efrat lives in Israel, so we have never had the pleasure of meeting in person, but a deep and supportive friendship has formed online. Both being spiritual authors, we have shared stories, resources, and struggles. I adore her, and her work with mindfulness and spirituality around being a parent is so very important and needed during this time.

Biography
Efrat, Shokef, Ph.D., is the author of *The Promise We Made: Three Universal Soul Promises We Made to Our Children — Near Death Experience and The Parenting Teachings it Invites*. She is a mother, wife, daughter, friend, writer, cosmic journeyer, and guide to spiritually aware families worldwide. Learn more at: efratshokef.com and efratshokef.com/the-promise-we-made

DR. ENOLIA FOTI
I met Enolia through a group of experienced healers that both of us were invited to join. When we first spoke, we connected deeply and found our paths were so parallel that it was amazing we had not met before. Both of us were raised in NYC, both lived in the same area of upstate New York, both studied under some of the same teachers, and both of us remarried into relationships beyond our wildest dreams. Enolia is so very wise and offers many tools for mindfulness and empowerment.

Biography

Dr. Enolia Foti is a respected Grandmother, Elder, and Doctor, and a Modern Day Medicine Woman in Energy Medicine, practicing in Africa. With decades of experience, she uses a holistic approach to guide individuals toward balanced health, integrating ancient traditions into modern wellness practices. Enolia offers classes and retreats on Healing, Self-Mastery, Dynamic Meditations, and Conscious Mindset. Internationally recognized as a thought leader, Enolia is an award-winning keynote speaker, author, global influencer, and coach. She is dedicated to youth advocacy, women's empowerment, and contributing to Africa. She holds an Honorary Doctorate in International Peace Ambassadorship from the United Nations and an Ambassadorship for Human Rights from the World Assembly for Peace. You can visit her site to learn more about her services and books. enolia.live

JIM KUPCZYK

I met Jim when I became a seller on the Mindful Market site he founded, where conscious consumers can purchase products and services that align with their values. www.mindfulmarket.com. When we met, we formed an instant friendship, and he felt like a long-lost brother. We had a similar mission — to help others embrace self-love and self-worth to step into the best versions of themselves. He had almost completed his development of the amazing program, www.selfworthnow.com, and I was honored that he asked for my insights and we were able to finish it together. Jim inspires me with his love of helping others, kindness, and generosity. It was amazing to finally meet him in person and experience the amazingly healing ancient alchemical oils, Sahu Oils. We also created an oil together, "Intuition," which aides in going deeper in meditation. I know that anything Jim does, he does with his heart, and I feel blessed to call him a friend and to work in business with him.

Biography

Jim Kupczyk is a lifelong seeker, passionate about exploring the depths of human potential and raising collective consciousness. Born and raised in Buffalo, New York, Jim has spent over twenty years immersed in energy work, constantly refining his practice and expanding his knowledge of alchemy, peak performance, and the ancient mysteries of Egypt. A dedicated student of truth, Jim combines his love for photography and his understanding of the metaphysical to capture and share the beauty and energy of the world around him. As the founder of Sahu Oils, Self Worth Now and Mindful Market, Jim's mission is to help others connect with their higher selves, embracing a heart-centered approach to personal transformation. Through his work, he inspires others to step into their power and raise the vibration of the planet.

Learn more:
- Sahu Oils sahuoils.com
- Self Worth Now selfworthnow.com
- Mindful Market mindfulmarket.com

JUSTINE WYROSTEK

I was struggling so much after losing my mom. Justine helped me connect with my mom and to tap into powers I didn't even know I had. She is the most gifted medium I have ever met and a soul sister. Anyone I have referred to her has had a mind-blowing reading and has reconnected with passed on loved ones. She emits love and a deep care for helping her clients. She has been my spiritual mentor, and I feel so blessed to have connected with her.

Biography

Justine Wyrostek is an internationally known Spiritual Medium. She is a High Priestess in Wicca/Pagan. She offers Tarot Readings & Rituals as well as Trauma/Ancestry Clearings. She can be reached via her Facebook business page under Justine Wyrostek International Celebrity Psychic Medium.

MARGUERITE UHLMANN-BOWER

Marguerite has been a friend for almost two decades, and her love of nature and the planet has been a source of constant inspiration to me. We were both born in Brooklyn, and she also had a bond with my mom. She introduced me to the Music of the Plants machine (musicoftheplants.com) and so much more. A walk through the woods with her is always a soulful learning experience. I love our connection and the fun we have as friends with our hubbies too. There is so much to learn from Marguerite, as she guides you to connect with nature in deeper ways than you may have ever known possible.

Biography

Marguerite Uhlmann-Bower is a lover of Plants, Earth and Nature, Co-founder of Plant Pioneers, a human-plant relations collective, and a clinical herbalist. As an Earth School Educator, with permission, she speaks for and is guided by the voice of Plants and Nature. For over 35 years, she's been a radical wild forager, Plant medicine maker, Plant intelligence researcher, writer and program developer for their now primary training program, *Cultivating Cognitive Agility with Our Plant, Tree and Nature Allies*. She reflects: "As we recover and deepen our abilities to language with Nature, we Naturally remember, we are born relatives of this sacred place, Earth". See PlantPioneers.org for more info on trainings and join her monthly Zoom Cultivating Circles to practice Plant communication and the sense of deeper belonging with the Natural world.

SEANA ZELAZO

I met Seana a couple of years ago after reading her book, *The Way of Inanna: A Heroine's Guide to Living Unapologetically*. I was lucky enough to be in a book club with Sacred Stories Publishing where she spoke about her book, which had moved me so much, and meeting her felt like I had found a long lost friend. We connected outside book club, became fast friends, and even created an online class together. She was my inspiration for releasing my poetry book, *Soulful Alchemy*, and has been an absolute joy to be friends with. We have deep conversations, and our love and support for each other is felt in every interaction.

Biography

Seana Zelazo is an author, psychotherapist, intuitive channel, and spiritual coach. A licensed clinical social worker who holds a Master of Social Work from the Smith College School for Social Work, Seana began her counseling career in end-of-life care as a hospice social worker before transitioning into private practice as a psychotherapist. For the last decade, Seana has focused on providing clarity and support as an intuitive channel, connecting with the higher realms to offer guidance, spiritual coaching, and mentorship. Her book, *The Way of Inanna: A Heroine's Guide to Living Unapologetically* can be found at book sellers worldwide. Learn more about her at seanazelazo.com

RESOURCES MENTIONED IN THIS BOOK

The Prologue includes a reference to shamanistic teacher Karen Johnson. Learn more about her wisdom in her book: *Living Grieving: Using Energy Medicine to Alchemize Grief and Loss*, Hay House, 2021. karenjohnson.net

Masaru Emoto's work with water is mentioned in the Introductions of Chapter 2 and 3. Knowing how powerful words and water are together will only deepen your mindfulness practice in the shower. You can check out Emoto's work on YouTube or by reading his book, *The Hidden Messages in Water*. He has passed, but his work very much lives on.

God Talk by Neale Donald Walsch is mentioned in Exercise 15. I had my story, "The Supernatural Washing Machine," published in this collection, and it was truly an honor. This book was published as part of the Common Sentience Series by Sacred Stories Publishing. I highly recommend this book and ALL of the books in the Common Sentience Series. My stories have been featured in two others, listed in the section of this book, called "Previous books by Jenny Garufi."

Rumi's Poem, "The Guest House," was featured in Chapter 16 on Emotions. Rumi was a great Sufi mystic and poet in the Persian language and is one of my favorite poets. There is a lot to learn and inspiration to be gained by diving into his work!

As mentioned in Exercise 16, Brené Brown's work on emotions has been amazingly helpful for me and my clients. You can find out more about her work on her website. I highly recommend her TED talk on shame, as well as her book, *The Atlas of the Heart* and the associated TV series. Learn more at brenebrown.com

Affirmations — There have been many authors who have written about the power of different affirmations. I learned about the power of "HU" through eckankar.org. I learned about the power of the "I am so happy and grateful now that…" affirmations from the late, amazing Bob Proctor (proctorgallagherinstitute.com) and from the incredible Brian Scott. youtube.com/@BrianScott1111

Sahu Oils — These are sacred oils, some of the oldest in the world, from Egypt. They are also taken to a pyramid to soak in more healing energies. They are truly alchemical and can add to the bath and your shower experience. I am a vendor of these oils and back them with my whole heart. My good friend Jim is their exclusive U.S. carrier. You can visit my shop here: sahuoils.com

The Self Publishing Agency — For those looking for book publishing support, my team at The Self Publishing Agency can be your team, too. theselfpublishingagency.com

Photo: Jessica Marx

About Jenny Garufi

Jenny Garufi (formerly Mannion) is an internationally recognized author, speaker, teacher, and healing practitioner who knows firsthand the power of transformation. After healing herself from seven years of chronic illness in just three weeks, she was called to share the tools and insights that changed her life. For the past two decades, Jenny has dedicated herself to empowering others to reconnect with their inner strength, self-worth, and capacity for joy.

With a blend of warmth, humor, and deep compassion,

Jenny offers simple yet powerful practices that make healing feel natural, accessible, and even fun. Through her books, workshops, and one-on-one work, she helps people dissolve limiting beliefs, attract aligned relationships, and create lives filled with clarity, connection, and peace.

She believes true transformation doesn't require struggle — it begins with small, mindful shifts that ripple into every area of life. When she's not writing or teaching, you can find her hiking in nature, dancing in the living room, reading with a cup of tea, doing puzzles, sharing laughs with loved ones, or cooking up a yummy meal with her husband.

Visit jennygarufi.com for services as well as access to Jenny's free eBook, *5 Critical Tools to Reclaim and Maintain Your Inner Peace: An E-Course*. Jenny offers other recommended resources on her site to continue with your learning.

Other books By Jenny Garufi (formerly known as Jenny Mannion):

- *A Short Path to Change: 30 Ways to Transform Your Life* by Jenny Mannion — Published by Llewellyn Publishing in 2016
- *Soulful Alchemy: Transformative Poems for the Soul* by Jenny Garufi in 2024

In 2023, Jenny (Mannion) was featured in three compilations in the Common Sentience Series by Sacred Stories Publishing:

- *Signs* with Simran includes Jenny's story, "Signs from Mom."
- *Akasha* with Lisa Barnett includes Jenny's story, "Released from Ropes."
- *GodTalk* with Neale Donald Walsch includes Jenny's Story, "The Supernatural Washing Machine."

If you enjoyed this book and found it useful, then I'd really appreciate it if you would post a short review on Amazon and/or share it with another person you think would find it useful. I do read all the reviews personally, so that I can continually write what people are wanting.

Thank you so much for your support!